T0167145

Sinners
OR
Saints

Caroline

Order this book online at www.trafford.com
or email orders@trafford.com

Most Trafford titles are also available at major online book retailers.

Printed in the United States of America.

ISBN: 978-1-4907-0679-5 (sc)
ISBN: 978-1-4907-0678-8 (e)

Trafford rev. 07/02/2013

 www.trafford.com

North America & international
toll-free: 1 888 232 4444 (USA & Canada)
phone: 250 383 6864 ♦ fax: 812 355 4082

Contents

CHAPTER 1

My life began tragically and brutally. My mom and dad had a fight, one of many. After her brutal beating, she stumbled from the house in the middle of a terrible summer storm. My mother was in her 7th month of pregnancy when she lost control of her car and rolled over a bank. I was born weighing in at 4 pounds, 2 ½ oz., blonde hair and green eyes. Mom laid down the hall in the recovery room thinking about everything that had happened to this point.

My dad wanted to be a big country music star. When he met mom he was playing music in some honky tonk. She was dragged there by some of her friends that night after finishing her shift at the diner. This sort of place was not her thing. She was quiet, kind of shy, and not out going. She was more of a home body. She was a beautiful slender, green eyed, auburn haired Iris girl who put family first in all things. She believed in doing what was right and treating people fair. Dad was attracted to her and soon they started dating. He got a TV spot at a local station where he and his band played. Later he was offered a chance to do commercials. He thought he was something. He was the center of attention and he loved it. Mom couldn't hold a candle to his majesty. It didn't take long for his success to go to his head. However, pride comes before a fall. He was a big drinker and partier. When he had had to much to drink he would sometimes get violent. His drinking and his temper soon caused him to loose everything. His band fired him so he lost his spot on the TV show and because he showed up drunk for the commercial shoot he was fired from that to. Who was there for him? Mom. She loved him and she was taught that marriage vows were sacred. "Till death do us part."

I guess he realized that she would always be there. She bailed him out of jail, she gave him money when he was broke, she went without things that she wanted or needed just so he could have what he wanted. She knew his faults but she married him anyway. I guess she thought that the responsibility of being married and a family would settle him down. Soon after they married he started to change and not for the good.

His drinking got worse. He couldn't hold a job because of his past record of violence, he would take long drinking bouts with his friends and she wouldn't see him for weeks. He would come home long enough to take his anger about his past out on her and have forced relations and then leave again. (Forced relations is now known as spousal rape). She was so embarrassed when the police would bring him home on Sunday mornings after picking him up off the tracks where all the drunks stayed the night before. Everyone that lived in that community knew that was the routine. I guess it was the City's way of "cleaning up the streets" on Sunday morning.

She shuddered as she remembered the events that happened just hours before. She was pregnant with me when dad was sent away to jail for the brutal beating of a man. She had not told him about me for fear of my life and her own. He didn't want children, not the ones he had and certainly not another one. Some how he had found out and that night he had come back to end my life and hers. She remembered the knock at the door and when she asked several times who it was there was no answer. She walked slowly to the door and suddenly it flew open knocking her backwards. It was dad. The look that night in his eyes was like none she had ever seen. They were full of hatred, anger and rage. There were so many questions going through her mind. How did he get out? What was he going to do to her? She backed away from him, scrambling on the floor. She started to scream and plead with him not to hurt her but she knew that he would not hear a thing she was saying. Now groggy from the anesthetic she tried to stay awake but she couldn't. Giving in she closed her eyes.

When she awoke again she saw tubes and heard equipment running. She had something in her throat. It was a nasal tube. She tried to move but realized that she had been restrained because of her injuries. Her baby? What about her baby? She tried to feel her abdomen. Her movement set off the alarms and soon nurses were every where. With tears in her eyes she mustered the word baby. "Your baby is fine, said one of the nurses. It's a girl. She is tiny but perfect. Now you have to be still." Smiling the nurse patted her hand and left the room. She was in so much pain. A nurse came in and sedated her so she could rest.

Lying there a few days later she saw a man outside of the Intensive Care window. He looked familiar but she couldn't see that well. The man turned around and started into mom's room. It was the lawyer that sent dad to jail the first time. He told my mom that he was sorry about what had happened. "Is there anything I can do? Is there anything you need?" Mom looked at the man with tears in her eyes. "Why did he do this to me?" The man was unsure and uneasy how to answer. The doctors had told him how fragile she was so he had to choose his words carefully. He told her that dad would not be hurting her again and that this time he would be gone for a long time. The lawyer had been a friend to her through dad's last trail. He knew in his heart that she deserved some answers. He gently took her hand in his and began with what he knew. "Some one came to visit him in jail and told him about the baby. He was told that the child was not his and the man that he beat up is supposedly the father. When he was scheduled for leave he told the Probation Officer that he was going to visit his sister. They verified it with her but when time came for him to check in he didn't. After calling the sister back, we found out that he never showed up. "Who? Who went to see him?" The man hesitated and said that he wasn't sure. He would check the phone log and see who requested to see dad. "You rest for now."

The days seemed to go by so slow. One day the doctor entered the room and ask if she was up for some company. A few minutes passed when in walked a nurse carrying a pink baby blanket. Inside of course was me. A few minutes later the door opened again and in walked a Social Worker with my older brother and sister in tow. Their eyes brightened when they saw the blanket. "Come say hello to your new baby sister, mom said." Of course boys being boys, my brother had to add his 2 cents worth. "Another girl! Ugh. Can't we trade her for a boy? I want a brother." Every one laughed. My brother didn't understand what was so funny because he was serious.

Mom made up her mind that she was going to find out who caused all this trouble and pain. She was wondering why no one from dad's family had come by or called so she decided to call her sister in law Beth. When Beth answered, mom thought that she had hung up on her because the phone went silent. The next words that mom heard tore her heart apart. "I am so sorry about this, said Beth. I don't know why Althea said those things." "Althea!" She was dad's sister. She was the reason that mom and I nearly died. Mom slammed down the phone and cried. Why? Why? Why? Why would she do such a thing? She knew that when she was released from the hospital that she had to get as far away from dad and his family as she could. She had her children to think about.

With 2 older children and me she had her hands full. She worked at a sewing factory and took in laundry and ironing to make extra money. One day a man came to the house. I heard them talking about dad. He was saying that dad had changed and was ready to come home. He wanted to talk to mom and see if they could work things out. "There is nothing to talk about or nothing to work out said mom. No he is not coming here. You keep him away from me and my children." But for what ever reasons, months later mom told us that dad was coming home. It didn't take him long to start drinking. All he did was drink and push her around if she wouldn't give him money to drink on. If he was home, he was passed out in the bedroom or on the couch. When he did work he complained about having to support the "little bastards". He would really go off if she asked him for money to help with clothes or food for us children. He resented my mom for having us and resented us because he knew as a father he had to support us. If he didn't he could go back to jail. He hated us because he had plans for his life and we weren't in them. He blamed my mom and said she trapped him. He looked at his money as his. He made it and he was going to do with it as he pleased. He said that he wasn't going to support us and he didn't.

It didn't take long for the abuse to start. I shuddered to think how many memories I have of my precious mother laying huddled on the floor, her mouth bleeding, crying in pain from where he had kicked her, beat her, slammed her face into the wall. How many times she lay there begging him to stop. I remember hearing my brother and sister scream as he beat them so badly that they could hardly walk, but the worst was still yet to come. One night in a drunken rage he locked mom out of the house but kept all 3 of us children inside with him. Being the wee one, I wanted my mommy so I was crying for her. To shut me up and to make matters worst, he dragged me downstairs and put me in the closet behind the steps. I screamed even louder as he locked the door and darkness closed in all around me. "Shut up you little bitch," he yelled as he stomped back up the stairs. I spent the night in that dark closet with rats all around me. He made my brother and sister sit right beside him and if they made a move he knew it. The next morning they saw mom outside the window. She motioned for them to go unlock the door. They did as they were instructed. "Where is your sister, she whispered"? They told her I was locked in the closet. As soon as she opened the door and I saw her face I began to cry. " Shhh. Mommies' got you". She gently covered my mouth to muffle the cries until she could get us out and to safety. Quietly and quickly we slipped away from the house. She took me to a doctor because I had rat bites on my hands and feet. Mom had had enough. She knew what she had to do, so she filed for a divorce. When dad got his papers he contacted her and ask her to come and talk to him. I guess in her mind, she might have thought that the filing of a divorce would bring him to reality. She was wrong. She took me with her that day because she didn't have any one to watch me. That day is a day that I have never forgotten and never will.

They started out talking but then yelling began. I ran and hid behind the couch. That country song "The Little Girl" comes to mind. My dad beat her, he kicked her and choked her. He had gone crazy. I was crying and screaming from the behind the couch as I listen to the horrible sounds. I remember him saying " no one leaves me!" He told her that he would cut her up so bad that no one would want to ever look at her again. She was begging for her life that day. He was going to kill her. He came over to where I was. He pulled me out by my arm. I was kicking and screaming. He threw me against the wall. I landed beside my mother there on the floor. I could hear my mother telling me to run. "Please baby, run!" I couldn't. I was so frightened. I couldn't move. Then I heard the sound of breaking glass. My dad had broken a wine bottle and was coming at my mother with the broken neck part. She was begging, pleading for her life as he sliced her neck like cutting through a piece of meat. I saw the blood and screamed and cried as my mother's body slumped over on me. Neighbors had gathered outside and sirens could be heard in the distance. I jumped as the door flew open and policeman rustled my dad to the floor. The damage had been done. To me and my mom. I went into shock and was taken to the hospital along with her. My mother survived, thank

God but my life was changed for ever. While my mom was in the hospital, her survival uncertain, my dad signed the papers for us children to be placed in an orphanage and put up for adoption. At that time it only took one parent's signature and I know that he took great pride in signing those papers. He was finally going to be free of us. In his mind he was doing the right thing and I guess at the time it was the right thing but it was for the wrong reason.

We were placed in the custody of the State. One day I stepped off a school bus and right into the back of a police car while the neighbors and classmates watched. I had nightmares for a long time and still to this day I can not watch anything that has domestic violence in it.

CHAPTER 2

Mom recovered as I said and she worked hard fighting the system to get us back. She worked 2 jobs and moved to another town. She got a home and was really doing well, but she made one big mistake. She took dad back when he got out of jail after pulling only half of his sentence. Don't ask me why. I guess love dose make you do crazy things. He must have made a big impression on her. I had not seen my mom in the 3 years I had been in the orphanage but one day she came to see me. I ran into her arms crying. I was so glad to see her. My joy was short lived when I looked past her and saw dad coming up the walk. I started crying and ran back to my room. The shock of that brutal attack on my mom years before had impaired me to speak well. I had hardly spoken for 3 years. The doctors said it trauma and I may never speak well again. I wasn't allowed to go to school and I had special tutors. But doctors don't know every thing. One of the little girls in the orphanage had been picking on me. I guess because I didn't talk I was a easy target. We were playing ball one day and it was my turn to bat. She was standing on the side saying things like, "she can't hit it, she can't even talk. She can't do anything. That is why she is here.

Her family didn't want her. No body wants her". I swung the bat as hard as a 8 year old could. The ball flew back and hit her in the mouth. She screamed and dropped to the ground. Crying she got up and started towards me. I swung the bat again, hitting her in the head. Suddenly I saw blood. I dropped the bat and collapsed to the ground next to it. When I came to I was in my bed. My house parents Mama and Papa Stacey were at my side. I looked up at them screaming and crying I said "I'm sorry." They both held me in their arms. All was forgiven. The other little girl was not seriously injured. The doctors said that when I saw the blood it must have triggered something in my mind from that night. It was like I wanted to help my mother that night but couldn't because of my own fear. So when the little girl started saying all of those mean things, picking on me and hitting me I fought back. My husband says today that I must be making up for those 3 years because I love to talk to people.

To some of the girls I was a hero because that little girl was a bully. To her and her friends I was a threat and they were going to get even and they did. A bump on the head and a busted lip did not compare to the brutal abuse I would go through for the next 6 months. One night I was the last one to get a bath. I liked the back stall because it was private and secluded. I heard someone come into the main part of the bathroom up front but didn't think anything about it. When I started to get out of the tub someone grabbed me. I felt hands on over me pulling me to the floor. I saw 5 girls and among them was the girl I had hit with the bat. One of them held my hands, 1 stuffed a rag in my mouth and the other two each held one of my legs. The girl that I had hit with the bat raped me with a hair brush and toilet bowl brush while the other girls held me down. I tried to get away from them but being the smaller of them all and out numbered by 4 I couldn't. After it was other, they left laughing like someone had just told a joke. I laid there crying and bleeding on the cold bathroom floor. For several days I could hardly walk but no one asked any questions. I guess they thought I had hurt myself some how. This kind of abuse became a regularly occurrence for 6 months until the girls aged out and was moved to another dorm. I was to frightened to tell anyone, afraid that things would get worse. The rapes didn't stop with the girls. There was a small barn located on the grounds of the orphanage. The boys had been given a pig to raise. One day as I was leaving the barn from seeing the little piglets, I was pulled into some woods and raped by one of the boys. I hated that place, I hated those people, I hated those boys. Shortly after this I learned that I was going home. I was so excited. I was finally going to be with my mom again. The morning before I left I found out that my sister had run away from the orphanage. She had told someone that she would rather live on the streets than live with dad again.

After 6 long years I went home. It wasn't long after I got home that I realized that life in the orphanage was not so bad. I very seldom saw my dad except for weekends. When he was home I stayed in my room. I didn't want to be around him. My sister had moved back home for a short time. One night I heard arguing. I opened my bedroom door and stepped out into the hall way. I saw my dad and sister on the steps. Just as I stepped out I saw my dad raise his big hand and slap her hard across the face. Grabbing her by the shoulders he shoved her down the stairs. She landed hard against the wall at the bottom. At first she didn't move. My mother screamed and ran to her side. Slowly my sister opened her eyes and stumbled to her feet. She was crying and she turned to look at my dad one last time before walking out the door. I think that was when I realized how much I hated him. He turned and looked at me and I ran into my bedroom and locked the door. I slept on the closet floor that night. Outside my window was a street light and it shone under the door into the closet. I could see if anyone came in the room. The next morning my mother tried to make light of what I had seen. "They just had a disagreement and your sister fell down the stairs she said." I stared at her in disbelief. Why was she lying? Why was she saying these things? My sister did not fall. He pushed her! "Honey, you can't say anything about what happens in our house. I'm afraid if you do then they will make you go back to the orphanage. You don't want to leave mommy again do you?" She was asking a lot of this 12 year old child. So I had to keep quiet. I covered for a lot that went on in our house for that reason. I didn't want to leave my mom again. I was a kid. A scared little kid. I didn't know better. I did wonder if my sister would come back and if she didn't would he turn his rage on me? That answer came to quick.

CHAPTER 3

My sister left home for good. She got married and was living in Germany. My brother was married and living in Florida. That only left me. I was not a trusting person. Every one that I had tried to trust had either hurt me or lie to me. I was afraid of everyone and not a good judge of character. I had very few friends if any. I had one really close friend and the only reason that we hit it off is because she was going through the same thing. Because of my dad's reputation of being the town drunk, people didn't want their children to have anything to do with me. My dad was hospitalized 39 times in his life for alcoholism. My mom was always there to put things back together. When I started to high school it should have been a time of dates, dances, proms, homecomings and building a lifetime of friendships. Not for me. I was being abused at home and every time mom would step in she would be abused even worse. We had to be quiet about it to protect each other. This is a lesson I learned early in my life and had to practice it through out my life.

I was the only one at home and dad wanted me out of his house. He wanted to finally be kid free. But I didn't see that happening any time soon and he didn't want it any more than I did. I was a teenager but I wasn't dating. I was never asked out. So he knew he had to do something. He started "hiring" boys to take me out. You read right. He paid boys to take me out. Now you are probably thinking that I must have looked like a dog. Actually I was known as one of the prettiest girls in school. I was 5'6, 80 to 90 lbs. long auburn hair, hazel green eyes. I must have looked a lot like my mother in her youth. I was offer a modeling career when I finished high school with Fashion College, but that never happened because that took money. There were boys who wanted to ask me out but because of who I was they didn't. My dad was desperate and every time he paid someone it ended in disaster. I was almost raped twice by these "Paid Dates". One was a policeman's son and the other was a college guy. I was 16. What would I have in common with a college guy? My grandmother had come to live with us and I was happy and content to stay at home and take care of her. She and I spent many happy hours together. I would stay with her while mom and dad went too the store or where ever. He never took mom anywhere nice. His idea of dinner out was a chicken dinner from some take out place. My joy was short lived because they would always come back fighting and usually it was about money.

One day dad come in from work and I heard him asking mom if she had a recent picture of me. I thought to myself, here we go again. He's going to fix me up. Gathering all the courage I could find, I walked into the kitchen and told him not to fix me up with any more boys. "I am tired of you renting me out I said." He was furious. He slapped me hard across the face. "You'll go! And let me tell you something you little bitch. As long as you live in my house, you will do as I say!" I walked into my room and shut the door. I fell across the bed and cried. That Sunday I went on the "date" but found out that this one wasn't paid for. A guy that worked with dad had a girlfriend and she had a brother. He had showed my picture to him and the plan was put in place. This boy was really interested in me. That Sunday we went out for a drive. Double date of course. I was very shy and sat as close to the door as I could get. I didn't say 5 words starting out, but before the day was over I had laughed so hard my sides hurt. I hated for the day to end. Justin was such a gentlemen. He walked to the door and kissed my cheek. "I really had a good time he said. Can I can call you and we go out again?" "I guess it's ok." I really never expected to hear from him again. When he did call I was a little embarrassed. No boy had ever called me before. I was really surprised when he called for a 3rd, and even a 4th date. Time just seem to fly by when I was with him. We would go for long drives in the country, sit in the middle of one of his dad's cattle fields and watch the cows. I would sit in the barn and watch him milk in the evenings before he took me back home. Once we went on a picnic and he swung out on a rope and jumped into the river. I fell head over heels in love with him but I couldn't tell me about my life. I couldn't tell him about the abuse. I was afraid to. I was afraid that if I did he would break up with me. I couldn't let that happen. Two reasons. First and fore most was because I loved him so much and second I was afraid of what my dad would do to me. We dated from August to December. At Christmas Justin showed up with presents for the whole family. I was surprised when he said that the biggest gift was mine. Everyone watched as I opened the big box. Inside of it was other boxes. Then other boxes. Finally I looked at him and said, "Is all you got me was a bunch of boxes"? He laughed and said keep going. Finally I got down to this small box in the bottom. I opened it and there was a set of wedding rings. The diamond was a cluster with a solid gold band. I looked at the rings and burst into tears. I knew that he cared for me but I had no idea that he cared this much. To want to marry me. He slipped the engagement ring out of the box and onto my finger. I was so happy. For that day everything was perfect. All the bad things in my life were far away. When I returned that evening, things were back to normal. Mom and dad were arguing. What about? Me of course. I heard dad say that finally he was going to be rid of me. The sooner the better.

When things got really bad at home I would beg and plead with Justin to come back at night and get me and we would slip off and get married. Every night I waited, sometimes all night long I sat at that window, but he never came back. To me it was saying that he really didn't love me as much as he said he did. Now, years later I understand. He was a very special person. One who had great morals and values. He wanted us to have a home when we married and be financially set. All I could see was us getting married and me getting out of a bad situation sooner than planned.

CHAPTER 4

When dad learned that Justin was drafted into the service he snapped. I had 1 year left in school. We had plan to marry in June of 1975. Now with him being drafted it changed everything. He was going to be in the service for 4 years. Four years more that I would have to stay in dad's house. Dad was not going to have that. He was going to get me out of there one way or another. One night Justin and I were talking. We were talking about the future and getting married. When the conversation went to us getting married before he left and my staying with his parents he was totally against it. I started crying. He kept asking me what was wrong. I couldn't tell him. He took my hand in his and looked at me. "I don't know everything about you but I know that you have had a hell of a life." "You don't know the half of it, I said." "I know you have reasons to want to get married now but I think we should wait. We don't know what is going to happen. I want to put this behind me and start our life together. Please talk to me. What is going on with you? I know there is more than what you are saying." All I could do was cry. After Justin left for duty, dad started drinking. I didn't think life could get any worse. I was wrong.

One morning as I was getting ready for school the phone rang. Mom called me from the kitchen, "it's for you". I walked into the kitchen thinking to myself who could be calling me at 7:00 in the morning? "Hello, I answered". Mom turned suddenly when she heard me gasp. "Oh no"! Mom dropped her dishrag in the sink and had started towards me as I collapsed to the floor. She was calling for dad. He ran into the kitchen and picked up the phone. "Hello, who is this?" "Sir I am Father Meredith at the army hospital in Fort Knox. I am sorry for this call and I apologize for the time. Justin is very ill. Critically ill. His prognosis is not good. He is asking for your daughter. If there is any way possible can you bring her to him"? Mom was crying. "Let me see what we can do he said". Dad thanked him for calling and hung up. I was sitting up crying. "Can we go? Please mom". Mom looked at dad and he picked the phone up again. He called his work and told them what was going on. Soon we were on the road. All I could think about was getting to Justin.

We started making a lot of stops and dad was buying a lot of Nyquil. His driving got worse and worse. He was swaying all over the road. He and mom were fighting. I became frightened. I knew something was wrong. My worst fears came true when we pulled into a little parking lot and across the street was the ABC store. "Oh no, I said". Mom turned around and snapped at me. "Don't you open your mouth". I had never heard her talk like this. Was she afraid to? Dad got back in the car and turned up the bottle. I laid down in the back seat and cried myself to sleep. I was awakened when the smooth road went rough and bumpy. I sat up straight in the back seat. Looking around I screamed. I reached past dad and grabbed the steering wheel. My scream woke him up and he hit the brakes. Mom had fallen asleep and my scream woke her up. The car slid to a stop just before going over a bank. I put the car in park and sank back into the seat. My heart was pounding so hard and so fast. Dad had passed out behind the wheel. Mom climbed out of the car and slid into the drivers seat, ordering dad to move over. "Mom what are you doing? You can't drive. You don't have a license"! "Shut up. If it weren't for you, we wouldn't be in this mess"! I was shocked. My mother had never spoken to me like that. I sat back and started crying. She managed to get dad over to the other side of the car and soon we were on the road again.

About an hour later mom pulled into a store and asked me if I wanted anything. I just shook my head no. Shaking dad to wake him up she said. "Hey wake up. I am going to get us some coffee, I think I have gotten us lost". "Oh hell", he said as he straightened up. Dad drank the coffee and slid back into the drivers seat staring at me through the rear view mirror. It was 1:30 in the morning when we arrived at the military base where the hospital was. A MP (Military Police) stopped our car and after dad explained to him why we were there, he led us to a hotel that had rooms reserved for us. I was tired and so glad that I had a room all to myself. I took a quick shower and climbed into bed.

The next morning I was awaken from the sounds of a horrible fight. I jumped out of bed and listened. It was mom and dad. I was so scared and alone. I was here in this strange place, the first time I had ever been anywhere. I slid down the wall, huddled on the floor of that lonely hotel room, thinking back to when I was a child. I knew in my heart that things were only going to get worse. I dreaded the drive back home and I wondered if we would even make it with dad in the shape he was in. I brushed the tears away and got dressed. I walked outside my room and there was a small crowd of people standing outside mom and dad's room listening to their fighting. "Should we call the police? Someone asked". "No it's none of our business someone else said". They all seem to stared at me as I walked past them. It was like they knew I was with them. I kept my head down and kept walking to the car. After siting there a while I decided to go back to my room.

We had breakfast and went to the hospital. Father Meredith met us at the front. He extended his hand to dad. I knew that he smelled the alcohol on him. He looked past them and right at me. "I need to talk to all of you before you see Justin. Please follow me". We sat down in this waiting room and he began telling us about all of the equipment that he was hooked to. He said that we had to be very careful not to hit or touch any of it. I felt like he was saying this to dad because of his drinking.

He told us that his condition was still listed as critical. We could only stay for a few minutes. As I walked into the room I thought to myself, this must be a mistake. This can not be him. When I got to the side of the bed and I saw his face, I knew it was. My heart broke. He was so small and fragile. He opened his eyes and looked at me. I was afraid to touch him. I reached out and touched his hand and he opened his eyes again. He had a nasal tube in so it was hard for him to talk. Our conversation consisted of a yes nod or a no nod. I didn't know where my parents were and at that time I didn't care. I was with Justin and that was all that mattered. The door opened and in walked mom. She stayed for a few minutes and left again. When it came time to leave Justin managed a few words. "I know. Be careful. I love you". Trying hard to hold back the tears, I couldn't. I cried so hard it nearly took my breath away. I didn't want to go. I didn't want to leave him. I thought that the next morning we would go back to the hospital but dad headed out for the highway. "Where are we going? We are suppose to go back to the hospital, I cried". "You've seen him and now we are going home, said dad". Justin was expecting to see me again. What would he think? I never said a word all the way home and went to my room and cried myself to sleep. The next day the phone rang and it was Father Meredith. "I am calling to check on you, one for Justin and the other for myself". "I am sorry we didn't come back. My dad wanted to get home". "I know what is going on and Justin dose to. I can't do anything about your situation but please find someone to talk to. A safe place to go to if you need it. I will tell him you are ok". "Father. Tell him I love him". "I will, but he knows that. Take care my child".

After we got home things went from bad to worse. Within the months to follow dad brought all kinds of false charges against me. Prostitution, drugs, contributing. He was told that the maximum sentencing for first time offense for these charges would be for me to be sent away until I was 21. That is what he was pushing for. While waiting for a court date for the charges, I worked in a drapery department in a store across town making $21.00 a week. I managed to buy a hope chest and started buying things for mine and Justin's home. I went to school and took care of my grandmother. My heart and mind were filled with thoughts of marriage not considering the outcome in court. I had been going to church and one night I had gone to a play with a girl from school. I told mom that if something happened and they didn't pick me up I could get a ride with the girl and her brother. That night mom and dad never came to get me. The girl's brother was taking his girlfriend home (she lived behind the church) and when he came back by I was still sitting on the church steps. He asked me if my parents were coming and I said, "I guess not." He gave me a ride home and as we pulled up in front of the house, my heart sank. There was no cars, the front door was standing wide open and where was my grandmother? "Oh No!" I jumped from his car and ran up the steps. "Hey! What's going on? Slow down! You are going to fall! came the boy's voice behind me." "I have got to get to my grandmother, I yelled!" I ran into the house and I was so embarrassed! There was beer bottles and wine bottles sitting everywhere. Ash trays had been knocked over. Dinner plates knocked in the floor and left. It looked like there had been another fight. My 99 year old grandmother was in her wheel chair in front of the TV. I knelt down in front of her slowly, so not to startle her. The boy that had brought me home had reached the door and stopped in his tracks when he saw the mess. "Woe!" I asked my grandmother where my parents were and she said that they had gone out a while ago. Suddenly I heard someone at the door. I ran to open it thinking it might be my parents and that they had left their keys. I opened the door and there stood Justin! He looked past me and at the boy standing in my living room. Then he looked at me with such hurt in his eyes. I started to cry and he just walked away. I was so embarrassed and so ashamed. I could only imagine what was going through his mind, but my main concern was my grandmother. The boy that was there said something about leaving and walked out. I gave my grandmother her meds and put her to bed. I was so scared. What if something happened to her during the night? I crawled into bed and cried myself to sleep. As I laid there all I could think about was Justin's face and what he must have thought. Had I lost him for good? Would he let me explain? What would I say?

The next morning my parents came in. Dad was still drunk from the night before. He had been invited to a party and they decided to spend the night so he wouldn't be driving. Suddenly there was a knock at the door. When I opened the door Justin only said 6 words. "I came to get my rings." "Please let me explain." He turned and walked to the other side of the porch. He couldn't even bare to look at me. I went and got his rings and placed them in his big hands. I stood there and watched him drive away, as tears rolled down my face. At that moment I was so hurt and so angry. I walked back into my room, almost like being in a trance and got some clothes. "I guess he found out what a whore you are, said my dad." "Go to hell! I screamed at him." He hit me hard and I fell across the bed. From somewhere deep within me I found strength I never knew I had. I crawled back across the bed, my mouth bleeding and I hit him as hard as I could. He stumbled backwards. He got his balance and grabbed me by the throat. "Do it! Do it! I screamed at him. Kill me! Put us both out of our misery! You will finally have what you want. Me out of your life and you out of mine! Do it!" For some reason, he let me go, but before I could turn around he hit me again. "You think you are so tough? I will put you in hell before you raise a hand to me in my house. This is my house and you will do what I say you little bitch." He reached for me but I ducked and ran out of the room. I grabbed some change that was on the table and ran out the door and down the street. My sister and her family had only been back from Germany for a short time, so I went to a pay phone and called her. My brother-in-law came and picked me up. "Oh my God, he said when he saw my face." I was bruised, bleeding and my head hurt. When my sister saw me, she fell apart. I hadn't been there an hour when the police showed up looking for me. They took one look at me and said that they were going to file a abuse report. During this time dad had called who ever and told them that I had run away and was out of control. He told them that I attacked him and he wanted me picked up and put in jail. He asked that the hearing for the charges be moved to that Monday and it was.

That night the phone rang at my sisters house. It was Justin. He wanted to come and get me and we would talk. As I stood there holding the phone, I thought about all those nights I begged him to come back and he wouldn't. I thought about what I was facing on that Monday. I struggled in my heart and mind what was the right thing to do. Do I tell him and face him walking away from me forever? Would he wait for me until I turn 21 if they sent me away? Would he even want me after he heard all of this? I heard myself speak. "No. Just forget about me and go on with your life. Just be happy." I dropped the phone and sank to the floor sobbing. My sister held me in her arms. "I had to let him go, was all I kept saying."

CHAPTER 5

Monday morning came and I was at the court house waiting to be called. My mom was there but my dad wasn't. She told me that my grandmother had passed away during the night and that dad was taking it hard. When they called my name and I walked into the court room, you could have heard a pin drop. The judge looked at me and asked what happened. My mother stood up and said "she fell." The judge told her that he was not speaking to her. I explained what had happened. While I was talking a lady handed the Judge a sheet of paper. It was a copy of the police report that the officers took at my sister's house. The Judge asked where dad was and someone told him that he had signed himself into an alcoholic ward. Like in the Bible, the Judge looked at me as asked, "Where are your accusers?" He dropped the charges and gave my custody to my sister since I was only 17. How convenient. My dad signed himself into the hospital so he wouldn't have to face his lies. He was there for 2 weeks and since he signed himself in he could sign himself out. He wasn't completely "dried out" and when he heard that the courts dropped the charges he started causing problems again. He started calling my sister. Threatening her and her family. I couldn't stand it any more. Dad had 1 more shot at me. He called one night and I happen to answer the phone. (Breaking his restraining order) "Have you read the paper?" "No why should I?" "Let me read the obituaries.

Justin's name was all I heard. I sank to the floor dropping the phone. Within seconds my sister was at my side. She finished the conversation with our dad and hung up. Justin was gone. My beloved. I just wanted to die. My heart was broken. I was numb. What had happened? My sister told me that it was an accident. I was in a fog it seem like for several days. I thought to myself maybe it wasn't true. But No, not even my dad would be that heartless. I accepted it to be the truth and began planning my next move. Dad kept calling. I could not stand to hear my sister crying any more so during the night I left. I didn't know where I was going but I had to leave so my family could have peace. I knew that as long as I was there dad would continue with his harassing.

I hitched a ride to the next town and walked the streets all that next day. That night it rained and stormed. I was cold and wet. I found shelter in a door way of a store. I tried to stay out of sight of the police. I was afraid that they would make me go back home. Do you believe in Angels? I didn't but I do now. That night an officer woke me up by gently shaking me. "Hey little lady. What's your name?" "Why?" I asked with a tone. "That's a funny name. Let's try this again. Where are you from?" I didn't answer. I just shivered from the cold so he reached out to help me to my feet. I pulled away from him. "It's ok, he said. No one is going to hurt you. Let's go get you out of this rain." "Where?" He pointed across the street. It was the Police Department. So much for trying to stay out of the sight of the law. We walked across the street and into the big building. There he gave me some hot chocolate and a warm blanket. Back then the cops were the good guys. I didn't answer his questions and I kept dozing off, so he took me into one of the offices and let me sleep on the couch. That morning he woke me up with a biscuit and a soft drink. He had a kind face and didn't press for answers. He asked me how old I was and took me to see a Social Worker. When they said something about taking pictures I ran. I was a minor. I was not going back home. Anything was better than that. I hid most of that next day staying in stores and shops. That night I was back on the street. I saw a car go by and I thought I recognized the driver. He turned around and came back and sure enough it was a guy I had gone to school with. Rod was 2 or 3 years older than me. He stopped and we started talking. He really seemed nice enough but actions speaks louder than words. When we finished talking I started to walk away. "Hey, where do you live, I'll give you a lift?" "I don't have a place. I'll be ok." "Where will you sleep?" "Same as last night or maybe not." "What's that mean?" "A cop picked me up for sleeping on the street." He looked at me with deep concern. "Here, get in he said opening the passenger door. I will put you in a hotel for the night. As least you will be out of the cold." "No. I don't want anything from you." Before he could say anything else I ran off. Later that night as the temperatures dipped way down I second guessed my decision about that hotel room. The next day he came back by with food. For about a week we went through this. I was tired and desperate and very, very cold. One day as I was sitting in a park on a bench my brother—in-law happened to drive by. He saw me and stopped. He told me that my sister had not stop crying since I left. "Come on back with me. We will work out something." The car was warm and I must have fallen asleep because the next thing I knew he was waking me up at their home. Rod had given me his phone number to use if I needed to or wanted to.

It didn't take long for dad to find out that I was back. He started up again. I had to get away from all of them once and for all. I called Rod and asked him if he would come and get me. We went for a drive and I told him everything. "Your dad is nuts! Why dose he hate you so much?" I just shook my head. I didn't know. He could not believe the things that dad had done. He genuinely felt sorry for me. I told him about my plans to be married and what had happened. "What are you going to do now, he asked?" "I don't know, but if my dad has his way I will be sent off until I am 21." "Unless you get married?" I looked at him like right. "Who am I suppose to marry?" "Well, you could marry me." I looked at him with questions. "That's crazy. I don't really know you. I mean you seem like a nice guy but I don't know you. And beside you don't marry someone just to get out of a bad situation. (Call that statement ironic) You marry them because you love them and want to spend your life with them." "Well I do care about you." Feeling the tension he said, "and I did feed you for about a week. That's an investment." We both laughed. "I do miss you, now that you are not around. Besides if you change your name, your dad will not be able to find you." "That's true." "It would solve the problem he said." "What if it doesn't work out?" "Stop thinking negative. Besides have you had any better offers today?" Again we laughed. After talking for several more days and dad calling every chance he could, I made the decision to marry Rod. I thought that it would solve everything. Bad! Bad! Bad! Decision.

CHAPTER 6

I didn't know him but I saw a way out. I wouldn't let him touch me and he seemed ok with it for about a week. One weekend he had a party and had some of his friends over. That night I saw a side of him I didn't like or didn't trust. I found out about his drug habit among other things. As the night went on I became more and more afraid of him. In the early hours of the morning I was awaken but some one tearing at my clothes. I couldn't fight him off and there was no reasoning with him. After it was over I ran into the bathroom and locked the door. I sat there in the floor, hurting and bleeding. Of course he apologized and said it wouldn't happen again but it did. I lost a lot of respect for him and even began to hate him but I was trapped. What had I done? I had no way to leave, no money, nothing.

One day we took a drive. As we were going through town I saw a car. A car that I knew quiet well. The closer it got I saw the driver. Justin! I began screaming and crying. Rod thought I had lost my mind. He pulled over. "He's alive! He's not dead!" "Who are you talking about?" "Justin! We just past him!" " He is dead said Rod!" "No, No he isn't." At that moment Justin drove by. "Follow him, I screamed. Follow him." Rod started up the car and followed the car in front of us. Justin pulled up to the cattle guard at his house. He walked over to the car and Rod began to tell him the story. Justin opened the car door and knelt down beside me. "You're alive." Tears flowing down my face. "Yes. I am alive." He told me that he had moved on with his life. After we talked for a few minutes Rod pulled away from his house. I went into shock. For three days I did not speak. How could my dad lie to me like that? I hated him. I hated him so much. About a week later Rod went off the deep end. He hit me so hard I went through the front door out into the yard. He was sitting on my chest beating me in the face while the neighbors watched through their windows. Suddenly someone pulled him off me. I remember hearing punches thrown and a scuffle. Next I was being scooped up and placed in a vehicle. I would loose conscious and then briefly come to. I heard a man's voice telling me that I was going to be alright. Then I felt the car start up and speed off. The next morning I awoke in a hospital. The man was at my side. I recognized his voice. I tried to focus and look at him but my eyes were swollen almost shut. I could tell that he was a older man. Dark hair and dark skinned, like a tan. He spoke softly as he held my hand. "Hey there. How do you feel? Stupid question. You feel like a life size punching bag." I started crying. "I know it hurts, he said. Just rest." I lay there asking myself what I had done in my life that was so wrong that I deserved this?

I had jumped out of the frying pan and right into the fires of hell with Satan himself. Then I heard the man's voice again. "You rest. I'll be back later." I just nodded and drifted off to sleep. He did come back. His name was Edwin. I pressed charges against Rod and since we had only been married for about 2 months I had the marriage annulled.

When I was released from the hospital Edwin was there. He brought us milkshakes and we drank them parked beside the river. "What will you do now, he asked?" "I don't know. I guess I am back on the streets. I don't have a job, no experience, no car, no license." "Well I have a job offer. I am moving to the next town into a big house and I need a house keeper and a part time baby sitter. I am divorced and I have 5 children. I get 2 or 3 of them every two weeks. What do you think?" "What are you expecting from me?" "Nothing. This is a job offer and nothing more. I have been promoted and I will be attending some rather large events and dinners. If I need a lady on my arm and you are interested, then we will see how it goes. Fair enough? Besides, you can't beat the pay. Free room and board, all the food you can eat, heat in the winter and cool in the summer." I stared out of the window. Considering my options which I had none I spoke. "When do I start?" "I'll have to put you up in a hotel until the house is finished and settled. Then I will make the move. It will take about a week or two. "I shook my head o.k. When everything was final, I moved into the big house and everything was just as he promised.

CHAPTER 7

I was introduced to Congressman, Senators and Governors. I was dressed like a princess, wore expensive jewelry, rode in limos and treated like royalty. I was a modern day Fannie like the song. Edwin made it perfectly clear to all of the men everywhere we went, Hands Off! He never left my side and treated me with the up most respect. I was living a rags to riches life. Although I was almost 18, I could pass for 21. We went to high dollar night clubs that catered to private parties for everybody that was somebody. Life was very good. I sang one night with the band and had a great time. Every time after that that we went there I was asked to sing. Edwin didn't like it when they offered me a position with the band. "It's them or me he said one night." That was not a choice. I stayed with him, a sure thing. Things began to change. I thought that it was because of the attention that I was getting but something told me it was more than that. One night we had a terrible fight. Thinking back on that night I could see how Julie Roberts felt in Pretty Woman. As time went on I realized that I had fallen deeply in love with Edwin and he with me. When he asked me to marry him I was on cloud nine. Little did I know that all of my dreams were about to be shattered.

Rod had not given up on me. He had been trying to get me back. He had even tried to break in on me while Edwin was at work. The police was called and I took out a restraining order against him. One day out of the clear blue my mom called and invited us up for Sunday dinner. I am not stupid. Why was mom calling after all of this time? How did she get our number? I talked it over with Edwin and he decided to go. "Don't worry he said. If anything happens, we will get up and leave." "Why are you so calm about this? How did she find me after all of this time?" Edwin finally broke down and told me that someone had been asking about me. He told them that I was staying and working for him. At that time there were door to door Insurance salesmen. One had come there recently and Edwin knew him. I remembered them talking outside, and now I was being invited to my parents home. "O.K. listen. The insurance guy that came to the house is a friend of mine, said Edwin. He heard somewhere that you were here. He is also yours parent's insurance man. When he came here it was partly to confirm that you were here and partly to get information for your parents. Do I think something's up? I don't know. Maybe they just want to see you. Maybe they want to make things right. Either way you are safe with me. Nothing is going to happen." I didn't believe him. For the first time in a long time I was afraid. That day I begged Edwin to cancel but he refused. He was the kind of man who believe everyone deserved a second chance. He believed that there was always hope. We had no idea what we were walking into.

We pulled in front of my parents home and a sick feeling came over me. I did not want to go in there. Mom had assured me that dad would not be there. She said that he was back in the hospital. When I knocked on the door I heard my mother's voice say come in. As I opened the door the first person that I saw was my dad! I knew something was up then and there. Why had mom lied? I sat down in the chair closest to the door and Edwin sat in the one across from me. Mom never came out of the kitchen. I never saw her that day. We had not been there for more than 10 minutes when I heard a car pull up outside. I recognized the sound of the car and knew who it was. Fear gripped my heart. I jumped to my feet and screamed at Edwin. "It's a trap! Let's get out of here! Rod is outside!" Just as Edwin was rising out of his chair, dad pulled a rifle out from under the couch. He pointed it straight at Edwin and told him that if he even batted an eye he would kill him. Edwin's face turned white with fear. We both sank back down into our chairs.

I was afraid that if I didn't do what dad said he would kill Edwin. Rod came up on the porch and jerked the door open. Dad looked over at him and laughed. "See son, I told you it would work." "Why, I asked? Are you out of your mind? You don't know what you have done. You are going to get me killed!" "Oh so dramatic dad said. He isn't going to hurt you, the man just wants to talk to you. Now unless you want your boyfriend's brains to be scattered all over that wall, you will go with him." I looked at Edwin as tears streamed down my face. Rod grabbed me by the arm and then pointed a gun at the side of my head. When Edwin saw the gun his first instinct was to grab it. "No! I screamed." Rod pulled me toward the door and lowered the gun to the middle of my back. He told me that if I tried to run he would shoot me in the back. I was so frightened I could hardly walk. He pushed me into the car and demanded me to slide over. He started the car and drove across the mountain and out of town.

Dad held the gun on Edwin while Edwin tried to reason with him. "I guess you know that you just signed your daughter's death certificate, said Edwin." "You don't know what you are talking about, said dad. If you had stayed out of their marriage they would still be together. He told me all about it." "Well did he tell you how he beat her?" "He said that he never laid a hand on her." "I guess you believed him?" "That man sat here and told me all about it, said dad." "I can prove anything that I say to you about this, can you? asked Edwin." " Shut up, shouted dad. We'll see who's right. He'll bring her back in an hour and you will see I was right." "He will hurt her and maybe kill her. I hope you are man enough to handle the consequences if he dose. I hope that you can handle it when they come and tell you that your daughter is dead because of you." "Shut up!, shouted dad." Edwin didn't want to push him. He could see that dad was getting agitated. They had been talking for almost an hour and dad had been watching the clock. As the time came upon the hour, Edwin knew that dad was about to loose it. "Where is he? He said." "Edwin asked, yea, where is he? I tried to tell you. For God's sakes man, put that gun down and let's call the police. Let's try to find them and pray it's not to late." Dad began shaking as he lowered the rifle to the floor. Edwin jumped for the gun and then for the phone. Sometime during the hour mom had come out of the kitchen and was sitting in the chair that I had sat in. She was crying because she was sure that I was dead. She told Edwin that she did not want any part of this but that he made her do it. Her face was black and blue from where he had beat her because she didn't want to go along with the plan. If I was dead she was partly to blame. Edwin dialed the operator and asked for Police Dept. (This was way before 911). When the dispatcher came on the line, Edwin told them what was going on and gave them the address. Within seconds the police were there. They took the report and put a out a all points bulletin on Rod's car. Edwin and dad left together in dad's truck looking for Rod's car. Mom stayed at the house in case I was to call. The long day and a half search had began.

CHAPTER 8

Rod brought the car to a stop across the mountain on a deserted road. I sat against the door shaking with fear. He was talking about our marriage but I didn't understand anything he was saying. At least not until I heard him say, "If I can't have you no one will." I was wearing a beautiful cameo necklace that Edwin had given me. Rod saw the necklace and jerked it off my neck. He smashed it with the butt of the gun and then threw it out of the window. He became violent because I wouldn't stop crying and I wouldn't talk to him. He jerked my long hair and pulled me over next to him. He laid the gun on the dashboard and kissed me hard. I tried to fight him off but he was to strong. I could feel his hands around my throat, gently squeezing. I was afraid that he might strangle me so I quit struggling. With one last thought of hope I saw the gun out of the corner of my eye. I pushed with all my weight against his body and reached for the gun but he was faster. He grabbed the gun and smashed it hard against the side of my head knocking me unconscious. When I came to I felt something running in my eyes. I realized that it was blood when it dripped onto the seat beside my head. Rod had tied my hands to the door handle in the car and was tearing at my clothes. I tried to rustle away from him but I could not stop his brutal rape. He became angry and started hitting me over and over again. I past out from the assault and the beatings. This continued for hours. At one point I felt him shaking me telling me to wake up. I sat up, my head was splitting and I was sick. I felt him trying to redress me and getting frustrated he stopped. He started the car and we started moving. I tried to raise up to get some idea of where we were but I couldn't.

"Where are we going I asked?" "Just shut up and don't worry about it." I laid in the seat, weak and hurting. Then I felt the smooth road turn into a rough road. I pushed myself up to try and see where we were. I didn't have any idea. Nothing looked familiar. At that point I was to weak to care. When the car stopped Rod raped me again. Then I saw the knife! He threatened me and said that if I didn't do everything that he told I to, I would die a long and painful death. Suffering from exhaustion he feel asleep on the other side of the car. I thought that this was my chance to get away. I grabbed my clothes and jumped out of the car. My legs buckled beneath me. I picked myself up and started running. I didn't know where I was or where I was going but I knew I had to get away from him. Suddenly I heard the sound of the gun go off. I cried out in pain as the hot, burning, bullet tore into my body. My life flashed before me as I felt myself sinking to the ground. I saw Justin and then Edwin. Their memories faded when I lost consciousness as I fell into a ditch.

I don't know how long I laid there. When Rod realized what he had done, he jumped from the car and ran over to me. He rolled me over and I opened my eyes thinking to myself I am going to die. When he saw the blood he became frightened. I wasn't moving and barely breathing. He laid me back down in the ditch and ran to his car. He had to get out of there. It was starting to get dark but he didn't turn any lights on for fear that someone would see his car. I don't think that he gave it any thought that there could be people living on that road, and his not thinking would cost him his freedom.

The next morning two little boys was walking down that same lonely road to meet their bus when they found my body. Scared and crying they ran back to get their house. Their mother kept them at the house while she called the police and their dad came to me. He rolled me over and felt for a pulse. I opened my eyes. I heard the sirens and I knew that help was on the way. "You are going to be ok little lady. Just lay still. She's alive he yelled at the police, but she is hurt bad." I kept coming to and passing out all the way to hospital. I felt as if I was in a trance. I could feel them loading me into the rescue squad. I could hear the sirens. I went through hours of surgery for internal injuries. My prognosis was not good, but I survived. Mom, dad and Edwin were notified that I had been found and it was not good. Mom and Edwin waited outside the operating room until they brought me out of surgery. I was put on the critical list. Mom knew that dad needed serious help. He had done some pretty bad things before but he had never went to this extreme and why? Why did he do this? I refused to see my parents and had a restraining order placed against them. Edwin would not leave my side. I recovered from the physical injuries but the emotional impact of those hours still burn in my mind today. It is something that you never forget. To keep from being convicted, my dad once again signed himself into the Mental ward for 6 months. Rod was sentenced to 10 years for kidnapping and assault. He was out in 5.

CHAPTER 9

After all this was behind us, Edwin and I were back to normal or so I thought. We had a dinner party celebrating my recovery. That night I heard some of the guys talking. "Wonder if he has told her yet?" "I don't know. If it was me I wouldn't want to tell her after what she has been through." "Yea, he is a real SOB for doing this to her." What were they talking about? Who were they talking about? Were they talking about me? Had Edwin done something? Oh yes he had. He and a co-worker had been fired for having relations with a woman while at work. He told me about it a few days later. Right after I had told him that I was pregnant. He exploded. I had never seen him like that before and considering what I just went through, he scared me to death. His words hurt worse than anything he could have done to me. "Pregnant? I can't support 5 kids, an ex-wife and an unborn bastard, he yelled at me." "What did you just say?" "You heard me, he yelled. Get out! After everything I have done for you and went through with you and you go and get pregnant! Get out of my house!" He walked into another room of the house and I sank down on the couch. I was crying and shaking. I don't know what I was thinking but I kept hearing his words and each time they cut deeper and deeper into my heart. I ran out of the house. I started walking. It was snowing, cold and I was pregnant. I don't know how far I had walked when a police car came up behind me. "Hey, called the officer." "What? I screamed at him." I turned around to see the same officer that had picked me up off the street when I first came to that town. He started towards and I collapsed in his arms. I came to in the hospital with him and his wife at my side. His wife was a Head Nurse. I told them what had happened and questioned about the baby. Patting my hand she said that the baby was fine. I spent the night in the hospital and the next day the officer and his wife came back in to see me. "Do you have any place to stay, the officer asked?" "No. I don't even have any clothes except these. I don't have anything. I just ran out of his house and started walking." I started crying and the officer told me that he was going to get me help. The next day a Social Worked came to see me and took down some information. Later that day I was taken to a trailer that the Social Service Department had found for me to live in. From time to time the police officer would stop and check on me but I never heard from Edwin.

On July 29th I had a 9lb baby boy. Someone had told Edwin I was in the hospital so he called. "So it's a boy? Well I guess one more son evens the odds. Three girls and now 3 boys." "Oh no, I cried. This is my son and my son only. You stay away from us. You have had nothing to do with me all these months. You haven't called or anything since I left. I carried this baby and delivered it with no one at my side. Don't think you can come around now and take up where you left off. It's not going to happen." "Listen, we need to talk, he said." "Go to hell, I yelled as I slammed down the phone and began to cry." When it was time to go home, the friendly police officer took us. I moved because I was afraid that Edwin knew where we were but he found us anyway. He demanded to see the baby and said he would get a court order if he had to. I had had enough to do with the courts so I agreed. As time went on he begged me to come back but I refused. He said I was keeping his son from him and if I didn't come back I would be sorry. He had friends in high places but I was still going to stand my ground. We never married so he sued me for custody and won. He used under handed tactics that I couldn't fight. He paid people to lie against me in court. He used my past (thanks to dad's information about the false charges) against me. When they took my baby out of my arms, I thought that I would die right there. I found out that 6 months later he gave my son up to be adopted. I hated him. He did this all because I would not come back to him. For months after loosing my son I had nightmares. I kept reliving them taking him out of my arms. The police officer's wife helped me get a job working at the hospital. I worked every minute I could to keep from going back home to the trailer that I had shared with my son. I bought a car. A fast car. One night after work me and some of the nurses went out for pizza. We all had a great time. I didn't like the road that I had to travel that night to get back home so I left early. Just as I started into a curb I heard a pop in the car. The car skidded back and forth across the road. I couldn't control it. The car flipped several times and bounced off bank. I was screaming as the car slid on it's top over a bank on the opposite side of the road. I was thrown clear at the sound of crushing metal that tore the car apart and just moments before the car burst into flames. The driver behind me stopped. He had a CB radio in his car and called for help. He climbed from his car and raced to where the car had gone over. He started down the bank when he saw me lying there. He stayed with me until help arrived. I was taken to the hospital again. When I woke up I hurt all over. They kept me sedated and I developed pneumonia. After a couple of weeks in the hospital I was back home. I wanted a change. My son was gone and I had no reason to stay in that area.

I moved away to start over. A few years had gone by when I met Darin. It had snowed and I couldn't get my car out so I walked down to the store below my house to get a few things. That's where I saw him. The owner of the store asked me what I was doing out in that weather? He said that if I needed anything to just call the store and he would have it delivered. I said that that was nice and I would remember that. As I started to leave Darin asked me if I wanted a ride. I declined and walked out. A few days later I walked back to the store and this time

I didn't decline his offer of a ride. We laughed so hard because he couldn't get up the hill either. I thank him for his kindness and walked the rest of the way. He found my phone number in the book and started calling me. Things were great while we were dating. We enjoyed just sitting out in the country talking. Just being together. We dated for about a year and got married. He became jealous. Very jealous. He made me quit work, he sold my car and then stopped my friends (what few I had) from coming to the house. He could have all the friends he wanted but not me. He stopped all my calls except to my mom. She was the only one that I could call. She didn't call often. If I wanted to use the car he would say things like, "if you want to use it then you have to put gas in it". Knowing I didn't have any money. He became violent especially when he was drinking. Martial relationships only happened when he had to much to drink. Again I became pregnant. Again I heard those horrible words "the bastard is not mine." He said that he wasn't going to support us and he stuck to his word. He gave me $20 a week to buy food for all three of us. If it hadn't been for my mom I really don't know what would have happened. Just like all the rest he wanted to hurt me and he did. He and dad became close and dad told him all about my past and the charges. In my dad's mind those charges were real and were still on record. One day I went to the store and when I came back I found Darin in the "act" with a girl he used to know. I took my son and left. I knew that I had to go back because everything we owned was there. When I confronted him about it, he slapped me. One day I was cleaning my gun and he came in in a rage. He grabbed me because I would not answer his questions. I knew what was coming. I had been hit for the last time. He grabbed me and swung me around to face him. When he did I pointed the gun right in his face. "Hit me. Do it!, I screamed at him. Give me a reason". He ran his fist into the door of the refrigerator which was to my right, backed away from me and left. As I lowered the gun it went off. I jumped. I thought the gun was empty. It startled me. Oh my God. I could have killed him! We had hired a contractor and we had a house built but a week before we were to move in, he left me. I came home from church one Sunday and there was a note that he had taken our son and left. The note also said that I wasn't worth the price of that house. I had signed everything over to him so that we could get the house and now it was all gone. He gave me one week to find a place to live and a job and he would let me have my son back. My mom helped me get a car and an apartment in another town. All that week I looked for a job. I went to the last place on my list and when they said no, I broke down right there in the office. The owner of the company called me into her office. I told her what was going on and she had compassion on me. She gave me a job and wrote out a note that stated that I was employed there. Come Monday morning I was given my son back. Darin was furious. He wanted to hurt me just like the rest. He asked dad to help him and of course he couldn't wait to hurt me again. We went to court and my dad's testimony sealed the deal. The Judge ruled in Darin's favor and again I lost another child. It also sealed the deal when he bribed my 7 year old son with everything he wanted. When he was asked who he wanted to live with of course he said his dad because his dad could give him things I couldn't.

A few years later I met Tyler. We were married briefly for a year and a half. We decided to give it another try, so we moved into a mobile home in the next county. One night I went to church. My heart was heavy. I felt like something wasn't right. I was suppose to do the service that night but asked the Head Pastor to do it. I left and went home to a dark house. I sat down in the recliner and at 1:00 the next morning Tyler came home. I had sat there thinking about my life. If this was really over I did not want to live. I did not want to start over again. I was tired of starting over. I went and got my gun and put it in the pocket of the recliner. I had made up my mind that if he told me it was over I was going to end my life right in front of him. I would give him something to remember. When he came in I asked him where he had been and he said that it wasn't any of my businesses. He told me that he hated me. He said that I was fat and he couldn't stand the sight of me. He said that I had 1 month to find a place to live and he wanted me out. I was so hurt and I was ready to end my life. I reached down and pulled my gun from inside the pocket of the recliner. I pointed it at my head. He froze. He said that he wasn't worth killing myself over and he was right. I didn't sleep that night and the next morning when he got up to go to work I started looking for a place to live. At the end of the week I was still there and he was mad. I had rented a storage building and started moving some things out but not fast enough for him. I went there one evening to get some of my things because it had started getting cold. I found my suitcases on the porch and the locks had been changed. I was homeless. I sat down on the porch in the snow and began to cry. I slept in my car for three days and on the church pews for 3 days. One day my mom and sister came to my office. Mom had called and called and got no answer. I told her what had happened. She was furious. My sister after years of living in Tennessee had moved back. She had a huge house and said there is plenty of room. I stayed with her for about three weeks and moved into my own place. After another failed attempt, I made up my mind that I was through with trying to have a successful marriage or happiness.

CHAPTER 10

I turned my heart to God. I started going to church and in October of 1989 I got saved. I spent my time at work or in church. Work, that's another part of this story. I worked in an office as the only secretary. I had heard rumors about the boss but I thought that I was tough enough to handle anything. Shortly after I went to work there, the boss said that he wanted to see if I could pass the pencil test. "What's the pencil test?" Smiling he walked over and dropped a pencil down the front of my blouse. "Oops, he said. I guess you failed." I took the pencil out of my top and broke it. Don't ever come near me again, I said." Laughing he walked off. "I like a woman with fire, he said." He was a jerk. He had a bad reputation for business. A real hard nose. One day he threatened me because he thought that I had said something outside the office that he didn't want repeated. "I know that you were the one that said it. Now let me tell you something. No one, no one is going to cost me my job. I will put you in hell first, he snorted." I stood to my feet and looked him straight in the eyes. "Are you threatening me? I asked. Because if you are you will be sorry." "I am just saying that if I find out that you did have anything to do with this I will fire you." "You don't have to. I quit. No one. No one threatens me I said." I stood up and got my things and walked out. He kept calling me every few minutes asking me to come back to work. I guess he was afraid that if I didn't have anything to do with it, I was mad enough to start trouble. I looked for other jobs but I couldn't find one, so I had to go back. When I went back he told me that now that I was back I was going to do anything he said. If I wanted to advance on my job I had to play by his rules. Wrong! Because I wouldn't play by his rules (read between the lines) I was denied raises and promotions. He would grab me and press me against the wall trying to kiss me. Several times men that worked there would pull him off of me. I was afraid to say anything. He told me/us constantly, "what happens there, stayed there." He threatened our jobs on a daily basis. We didn't dare say anything because everyone there needed their jobs. I was relieved when he moved on to the other woman that worked there. When I started out there I was making $4.98 per hour. When I left 20 years later, I was only making $19,000 a year, roughly $9.00 per hour. The other lady that worked there was making over $30,000 per year and she started 1 month before I did. He and I had our battles but by the grace of God I survived my 20 years.

After I got saved, I started singing in church. I had always loved to sing. I was invited to several churches to sing. My dad "found religion" in 1986. He was traveling and singing as well. I was glad to hear that he had changed his life. Someone signed for him to get his Minister's license although he had no formal training in the Bible. When I started taking courses in the Bible (just for knowledge purposes) my dad said that if I wanted to get my license he would see to it that no one would sign because of my past. I took courses for 6 years and graduated from Bible College top of my class. He did not like that a bit. He became jealous of my studies and my music. I was getting more bookings than I could handle. He didn't like it. He started telling people that he was my manager and if people wanted me to come and sing to contact him. When people called him, he would say things like, "I don't think she is available that night but I am." When they decline having him he would get mad. Mom would try to talk to him about it but he just got angry at her. He would slap her for taking my side. In 1992 I had to have emergency surgery for a tumor. After 12 hours of surgery and 6 weeks of recovery I was ready to get back out there and start singing again. People had started calling to schedule singings and dad started his lies again. He was so consumed with jealousy that he went into the churches and told them lies about me. He told them about those charges that didn't exist. I was questioned by one Pastor and their Board about the charges. When I told them that they were not true, they took my dad's side. "He is your dad and a Pastor. We don't think that he would lie about this." After the conversation ended I made a decision that I would finish out the singings that I had scheduled and then I would quit. The damage had been done and soon people were calling and canceling the singings. Once again my dad had destroyed my dreams. When the church that I had attended for many years questioned me and took a stand with dad, I left the church. I had been a member of that church for 12 years. My faith began to dwindle. I could not understand why God allowed dad to continue on this path.

CHAPTER 11

Then in 1996 I once again had to have emergency surgery for a ruptured gall bladder. I was air lifted to a trauma center in Northern Virginia. The first night there I had a mild stroke. Dad started making my funeral arrangements and I wasn't even dead. I was in the hospital there from December to March. Dad brought mom to see me one time for 15 minutes. Then he left and went to visit his sister just a few miles down the road for about 4 hours. When I was released I had to stay with them. I could not be left alone. I was only there 3 days when he kicked me out. He said that all I was doing was laying around, eating his food. I was to sorry to get up and help mom clean house or anything. I had 6 tubes coming out of my body. One night he went to hit my mom and I stepped in between them. He grabbed me and shoved me against the wall. In doing so he pulled two of the tubes out. I was rushed back to the hospital and back into surgery. When I left the hospital that time I went home. Home to a cold house with no heat no water and no food. Edwin and I had not spoken in years but he heard about my illness. He got in touch with mom and she gave him my phone number. One day he called and thanks to him, my furnace and water was fixed and he brought me some food. Even after I was better we stayed in contact with each other.

It was about this time that dad started seeing a woman in the church.

When mom confronted him about it he scowled her with a cup of hot coffee. Pastors would call mom and talk to her about it. When she tried to talk to dad about what was being said he would beat her. "I can do anything I want. My followers love me he said. At least I am not like that little bitch (talking about me) hiding behind the pulpit. Trying to hide behind the church. She thinks she has people fooled." Every time mom would take my defense dad would beat her. If he found out that she had talked to me on the phone, been to see me or had any contact with me at all, he would beat her. I could not stand it any more. I cut myself off completely from her to protect her. Even though I lived 25 miles away it wasn't far enough for him.

In July of 1997 Edwin called me and asked me if I was going to be home. He said that he had something for me for my birthday. He asked if he could bring it by and I said yes. A few moments later I heard a knock at the door. I opened it and there stood a tall, handsome young man. When I looked into his eyes I knew who it was. It was our son! In his hand was 2 dozen red roses. We all hugged and cried. We talked all that night and all the next day. Edwin said that he had told him the story about what had happened and I can only imagine what he was told. That didn't matter at that particular moment. I had my son there in my arms and I could not have received a better birthday gift. The following weeks were wonderful. We went out to the movies, out to eat, drove up on the parkway, watched racing, just spent time together. Then on September 4, 1998 Edwin called me and asked me to come and see him. When I got there I could see something was terribly wrong. "I didn't want to tell you this on the phone, he said." My heart broke at the news. Edwin was dying. He had found out in July (on my birthday) and that is why he brought our son to me. He wanted to make things right. He told me that he had always loved me and he was sorry for what he had done. I told him that he had always had a special place in my heart as well. I spent every minute I could with him and on November 12, 1988, Edwin passed away. My son and I have seen each other maybe a total of 3 times since that day.

In 1999 my precious mother went home to be with the Lord. Years of beatings and abuse were over. She was safe in the arms of her Lord. I was devastated. I had not only lost my mother but my best friend. We did not spend much time together the last 7 years of her life. When we did it was by chance. She had her friends bring her to see me. She would tell dad that her and her friend was going out and they would bring her to see me. She had to sneak around to see me because she knew that he would beat her if he found out. She loved the Holidays although they reeked with heart breaking memories.

Every Thanksgiving for as long as I can remember dad would start drinking. He would stay drunk straight through till March and most of the time he would end up in the hospital to dry out. He would beat my mother more during those months than any other time. One Christmas my phone rang and all I could hear was screaming and things being broken. I knew what was happening. I jumped in my car and drove as fast as I could to their house. I walked in just as dad was about to hit her again. I step between them and pulled my mom towards the door. I shoved her out the door and shut the door behind her. She was outside and I was inside with him. She was screaming beating on the door crying and begging me to open the door. I started towards him. I got in his face and begged him to hit me. "You think you are so bad. I am not afraid of you any more. Hit me! Hit me you SOB! You might hurt me, you might kill me, but I'm not going without you". I could hear the police at the door telling me to open the door. I lounged at my dad knocking him backwards. He fell. I turned to go towards the door to open it when he came at me from behind. As I opened the door, an officer pulled me out of the way. Dad fell in the floor. They got him up and hand cuffed him. I went to him and got right in his face and told him that he had taken everything that I ever loved away from me but I would put him in hell before he would take my mother. The officer asked me if I was threatening him. I looked at the officer and said, "No sir. I am promising him". They took him to jail that night but he was back out the next day. After he quit drinking the abuse still continue at that same time of year.

The weekend before mother passed my sister brought her to my house. The three of us went shopping and I bought her an Easter dress. I bought one just like it but a little different in color. She looked so pretty in the picture I seen of her. She was buried in that dress at my request and unknown to dad. She always said that she hoped when God sent his angels to get her that He would take her at Easter. It was her favorite time of year and the only holiday that she was beaten. She got her wish. She passed away the Monday after Easter.

The day we went shopping we stopped and got burgers. Mom hated dill pickles. My sister told them, "No dill pickles". Mom bit into her burger and started gagging. We started laughing and asked her what was wrong. She pulled apart her burger and was fishing the dill pickles off. She called them little sour boogers. These are memories I will always cherish. Another time mom and my sister went shopping. Mom did crafts and she had picked up a few craft things. Dad was with them of course and when it came time to pay he walked outside. Realizing that he was not going to buy her things my sister did. Mom was so hurt and embarrassed. People don't know this, but my mother walked the streets, stopped on the side of the road and asked people for their empty pop cans. She would take them to these recycling centers and trade them for money. My dad walked around with hundreds of dollars in his pocket and would not give her a dime. She and I opened a Checking and Savings account together. Every week I would try to put a little money in her account so that she could get what she wanted. I loved my mother with all my heart. I miss her terribly but I had to stay away from her to keep her safe. I know that people don't understand this and I know that my dad made it sound like I was doing it on purpose, but God knows my heart. He knows I would have done anything to protect my mom. Damn my dad for robbing me of those years. I had not had any contact with him since I came home from the hospital in 1997. Now that mom was gone I was truly alone. After her passing I hit my knees and asked God not to leave me in this world alone. I begged him to send me someone to share my life with. He answered my prayer.

CHAPTER 12

On 9-11-11 I went to hear a guy's band that worked with me. There was a guy that kept looking at me (I was informed of by my friend with me).

I looked over at him and recognized him but didn't know from where. I couldn't think of his name until someone said it. He and I had been friends briefly when I first moved to that area. As I was leaving that night I spoke to him and we talked for a few minutes. The next day he called me. Now this might not have seem unusual but my phone number was unlisted, and it had been seventeen years since I had last seen him. When I answered my phone I was shocked to hear his voice on the other line. "Hey there. How did you get my phone number, I asked?" "If you have dinner with me tonight I will tell you, he said." I said yes. At dinner that night, as we were talking, I asked him again how he got my phone number. He reached into his pocket and pulled out his wallet. I thought that he was going to leave a tip for the waitress when he pulled out a folded and faded piece of paper. He took the paper and gently unfolded it and handed it to me. I could not believe it. There was the paper I had written my number down on years earlier. I looked at the paper and then at him. "Oh my goodness. You held on to this all these years?" He just smiled and said, "some things are to good to throw away." Was this a sign from God? You think? I had my doubts but I was really impressed. From that day on we spent all our time together when we weren't at work. We had so much fun together and time just seemed to fly by. I denied I had feelings for him. Feelings other than friendship that is. For three and a half years I denied those feelings. Then he went away on a business trip and when he didn't return at the time that he said that he would be back I got antsy. I kept calling but there was no answer. A few minutes went into a half of a an hour, then an hour. I turned on the TV to watch the news and there was a special report about an accident on the same highway that he was traveling. As I sat closer to the TV I heard the man say that there were fatalities. I looked closer at the shots of the accident and there on the screen was a vehicle exactly like the one he was driving. "Oh my God!" This could not be happening. He could not be dead. I was crying and shaking. I could not imagine my life without him. Suddenly there was a knock at the door. When I opened it, there he stood. I ran into his arms and kept saying over and over, "I love you." Three months later he asked me to marry him. I told him that I didn't do marriages because they were hard on me. He just laughed. A few days later I sat him down and told him everything that is written in this book. He told me that it was time for a new beginning and he still wanted to marry me.

It's now 10 years later and boy what an adventure. He never told me that he was allergic to poison oak. One day I was cleaning out some brush from behind my house. I cut down a small tree and the wind caught it, blowing it back on me. He pulled into the driveway just as the tree started to come down. He jumped out of his truck and ran towards me, calling my name. Wearing only a pair of short and sneakers, not having time to put his shirt on, he grabbed the tree and was pulling it off me. A branch had penetrated my arm so we went to the house to clean out the wound. Within two or three days we both were covered with poison oak. I had to take shots because it got into my blood stream. We were miserable. I had told him about my gall bladder and how sick I was. Believe it or not, 2 years in our relationship and on the same day I had had surgery, he was operated on for gall bladder. His surgery ran into some bumps but nothing like mine. We were married in April of 2003 and on July 9th of that year I woke up not able to breath. I had gone into congestive heart failure. I looked at him while lying in the hospital and said, "See I told you marriages were hard on me." With tears in his eyes he just smiled. One year and two days later it happened again. I went through some test and found out that I had a valve that was leaking in my heart. MVP is what they call it. Diet, rest and exercise. The miracle cure for everything. In 2004 I took pneumonia. Ironically, his mother had it at the same time. Then in 2005 I took a horrible case of bronchitis. A short time later, he took it. We were joking one day when I told him that everything that I had had, he had had except for a hysterectomy. "I don't think I have that to worry about, he said."

CHAPTER 13

One night on September 4, 2006 the phone rang and it was my sister. "We just lost dad, she said." "I am sorry for your loss, but you know what I told you was my reply." "I know and as bad as it hurts me, I will do as you ask."

As a Christian I had to try and make things right with him before he left this world. So I had gone to my dad, knelt down beside him and asked him what I done to make me hate me so much. I begged him to tell me what to do to make things right. "I hate you , you little bitch. You have ruined my life. If you want to do something for me, don't be listed as one of my kids when I die because I don't claim you. Don't even show up at my funeral, because I don't want you there. Now get out! Get out of my house and don't you ever come back!" As I began to cry he shouted at me to shut up. He slapped me hard across the face knocking me off balance. I stood up and walked out of the house. As the door shut behind me, these scriptures came to mind. "Brush the dust from your feet." As if God himself were speaking to me, I heard these words, "Cast aside your hurt and pain and put him in my hands." I walked away never to return to that house. That was the only time that we had spoken since 1997. I broke down and cried but not for his passing but because he died without forgiving me. I never knew why he hated me so much. He said time and time again that he didn't need anyone or want anyone. He wanted everyone to leave him alone so he could live his life as he wanted to. In those last days the only one he wanted around was the woman he was seeing. The woman he had beat my mother and left her lying in the floor over. I was told that the night he was taken to the hospital he only asked for her. When they called her she refused to come. Although my sister and some of her children were there, he only wanted this woman. When they had him stable my sister and her children left. Within an hour he was gone. He got what he asked for. He died alone in that hospital. The woman that he had put above his own wife and children was not at his side. I did what he ask. I was not listed as one of his children and I did not attend his service. Although I know where he is buried I have not been there since his passing. At least in his death I feel like I did something right by filling his last request.

I have been judged harshly by people who knew him. I have been judged harshly by obeying his request. He was a Pastor but he was a true wolf in sheep clothing. The Bible says that in the last days that even the elect will be deceived. So many people that knew him were deceived by him. They thought he was a wonderful, compassionate, loving husband and father. They had no idea. This book is not to discredit him but to say to all those who praised him and in a sense worshiped him, "You did not know him." I remember one Sunday, a Mother's Day, we were leaving church. I had sang for my mom that Sunday. The Assistant Pastor, a large black gentleman came up and hugged my dad and told him that he loved him. When we got outside my dad jerked his jacket off and through it in the back seat of their car. " I can't stand for a damn N. to touch me, he said." "Dad, you just walked out of the house of God!, I said." He looked over at me and told me to shut up. He talked about other Pastors and was even threatened with a law suit if he didn't stop. "I'm just stating the truth, he would say." He thought that every one should know every thing that every body had done wrong but him. His past could not be talked about. That's not how God works. As Christians we are not suppose to go around digging up dirt on each other. Sadly that is how this world is. God can forgive, people can't.

CHAPTER 14

Thank God I have a husband who saw first hand how dad was. After we married dad even tried to cause problems for us. He told people that he knew that my husband had money and I only married him for the money. He said that my husband was a drug addict and he was my supplier and that he was one of my prostitution customers. When this rumor got back to my mother-in-law she called me. I went to talk to her and of course she knew that none of it was true so she sent dad a message. I don't know what that message was but I know that I didn't hear anything else from him. Now I know that you are probably thinking that all of this is here say. Wrong! Correction. Right. One day I went to the store. Now my appearance had changed. I had cut my hair and gained some weight since that last time I had seen my dad. As I was walking out of the store I heard a familiar voice. Yep. There he was. I walked right past him. I went to put my cart up when I heard him talking to someone. I heard it with my own ears. "No I haven't seen her but I heard that she's married again. I think this about the 4th or 5th time. Yea, I hear she is back on drugs and prostitution. It's sad. I love my daughter and I pray for her but what can you do? I guess since her mother died and she can't steal from her any more she had to find money some where else so she married someone with money. Just pray for her." I could not believe what I had heard. Standing right there in the middle of a store. I can't tell you of the times that I had people come up to me and tell me things he had said all to discredit me and for what? He had accomplished everything he sat out to do. I wasn't singing any more, I wasn't going to church in his town any more so why?

My husband and I have been together for fourteen and a half years. I have cut off all contact with my family. I have seen my brother maybe 4 or 5 times in 40 years. As a Christian and a Minister I wanted to try and fix this family. I did reach out to him but he didn't have the time to spend with me. So I deleted his email address, lost his phone number and remove him from my address file. I have done what I felt like God wanted me to do. I pray for him and his family but I can only do so much. My sister lives in this area. I have not spoken to her in 7 years. She says she is a private person and likes her privacy. I understand that. She has done more for me than any one else in my family. I will be forever grateful for all that she had done and the many times that she was there for me.

As I look back over my life it was horrific but I see the hand of God in all of these situations. As frail as I was as a child, my dad could have killed me easily but God didn't allow it. Yes I married a man for all the wrong reasons and I was wrong in doing so. Did God's punishment come in the form of kidnapping, torture, rape, being shot, being left for dead? That is not the God I serve. Was loosing my children my punishment for loving them? I think back on my life and I think of things that I have said. The Bible tells us that we have authority in our words. You can take authority over your life by the words you speak. As a teenager I said many times that I would not have children. I said this because I had no parental up bringing. My parents did not talk to me about things. Right decisions, choosing right from wrong. My childhood consisted of "Out of sight, out of my mind." No one on one with them. I also said that if I had children some one else would raise them. I meant that someone else would have to be their mentor because I didn't know how. Did these things happen? Yes. Edwin was a good man and father. He loved his kids. I found out later that although he gave our son away he still stayed in contact with him all of his life. He robbed me of that but in the end he brought him to me. He made right his wrong in my eyes. My dad? My mom and I talked one day and she helped me to understand some things but I believe that with the help of God I have figured out why he did the things he did. He wanted to be a big star but children got in the way. When he failed as a dad he took it out on my mom and us. He blamed us for all his faults and failures. He had to be the center of attention. He went to church because he knew that they would let him sing and perform. It was more of a show, act, performance than singing praises to the Lord. He only had a 7th grade education. He was jealous of my education, college and trainings. He had always struggled with money and when he got some he held on to it unless he could use it for some purpose to be recognized for. (Making big donations to churches, help to buy food for the hungry) If no one would brag on him for it, he would brag on himself. He had his own radio show. He bragged on the air about all he did for people and then turn it around to make it sound like he was doing it for the Lord. As long as he was the center of attention everything was good. When I started being asked to sing in place of him, he struck out. I was a threat to him. I was in his space. So he did everything he could to stop me and he did. When a scout came to town to hear me sing at the request of a country music legend, and I was asked to Nashville dad stopped that real quick. How. He was the told about the opportunity not me. Why? Because he was saying he was my manager.

When I became a Minister no one wanted to sign for me because of all of the things dad had told. No minister wanted their signature on that license but thank God one Minister didn't care. God has a way of working things out and putting the right people in your path. Give Him praise and Glory every day for the good and the bad. My dad was a mean man and I had a hard life. I made a lot of bad decisions and I take responsibility for them. The Bible says, "Let he who is without sin cast the first stone." So many so called Christians have cast their stones at me all because they listened to the wolf and not the Shepherd.

CHAPTER 15

We can not choose our families but the Bible said that God will give us families. For years after Tyler and I broke up I lived alone. Fourteen years to be exact. I was living in a trailer park. This man and woman moved in two doors up from me. One day she brought me a flower. She said "I don't know when you is but happy birthday." Another time they were having a cook out and she brought me a plate of food. Another time at Christmas everyone around me was either leaving to go to their families or their families were coming there. I was all alone. She brought me a little magnet to put on my refrigerator and some food. After I married and moved out of there we ran into them in a store. Now 11 years later, at least twice a month we still get together and share a meal and spend the evening. She had me listed as her daughter in case of emergency. She has no idea what she means to me. We share so many things in common. We both love gardening although she can't do much now because of her health. She has been there to listen and to cry with. Her husband is like the dad I never had. He is always willing to help in any way he can. I was honored when he asked me if I would take him to have eye surgery.

I could never repay the love they have showed my husband and I. I spend every Mother's day and Father's Day with them. I love them so much. God is true to His word. He gave me another family. Thank you Lord.

My husband. My wonderful, loving, precious husband. After 10 years of marriage he still thinks I'm the greatest. We still hold hands when we go out in public or taking a drive in the country. He still brings me flowers at least twice a month. He still takes me shopping every once in a while and buys me something. On 1-12-11 we lost his mother to Cancer. On 9-11-11 I collapsed after putting the last ceiling tile up in her house. We had no cell phones with us so he helped me to the car and we took off to the hospital. Upon arriving I was rushed back into the cardiac trauma center. My heart had stopped. When I opened my eyes I saw my husband standing across the room in tears. I was in the hospital for 3 or 4 days and he was at my side every minute they would let him stay. Physically I can't do what I use to do and I seem to be getting weaker every day, but he is there to help me even when I can't find the strength to keep going. We go to church on Sunday and thank God for another day. I love him so much. My hearts desire to have a big farm house style home in the country. He is working at getting me that while I can still enjoy it. Even if I don't get it, he has given me more happiness in the last fourteen and a half years to last a life time.

This book was written to give others hope. You may have had a horrible life but you can change it with God.

Your life is what you make of it. Don't let people or situations bring you down. Out of everyone that failed me, God never did. Yes bad things happened but I have control of my life now. I know the difference between right and wrong. I live by one rule, "Do unto others as you would have them do unto you." You treat others the way you want to be treated and you will be happy. God Bless all who reads this book. Gods blessings of peace and happiness on their lives. Amen.